Today's Lesson

Copyright © 2015 by Ralph Duncans Jr
All rights reserved.

Today's Lesson
Ralph Duncans Jr

ISBN: 978-0-9961766-2-0

This is an English language workbook

TABLE OF CONTENTS

From The Author	i
A and An	1
The	3
The/Which Do you want	4
Put Your Hands	5
The Days Of The Week	7
In Order	9
What Is Missing (PARTS)	10
The Months Of The Year	11
The Travels Of The Earth	13
What Are You Doing	15
What Did You Do	17
What Will You Do	19
Where Are You Going	21
Where Did You Go	23
Where Will You Go	25
How Many Sides	27
Where Are You	29
What Do I Need	31
Why Are You	33
What Are You Going To Do	35
What Will You Go Do	37
What Did You Go Do	39
What Do You Do On __Day	41
Where Is The (At) Singular Pt. 1	43
Where Are The (At) Plural Pt. 1	45
Where Is The (At) Singular Pt. 2	47
Where Are The (At) Plural Pt. 2	49
What is missing (Letters)	51
Do You Like	52
Basic Questions	54
Who And What	56

FROM THE AUTHOR

This textbook contains lessons I teach to my students in Japan. These lessons are taught in the order they appear. I write the words, questions and diagrams on a whiteboard using the same illustrations as they appear in this textbook. I say one of the answers for the students to choose after asking the question and/or giving instructions. Parents can use this book give their children an early start to comprehending English basics. If you are looking for a simple English book to teach your young children or young students, this is a perfect book to start with. If you have any questions, please contact me at my1english1@gmail.com.

"A" AND "AN"

"A" and "an" are very easy to comprehend and use.

1. Both equal to one.

    a. I see **one** ball.   I see **a** ball.
    b. I see **one** apple.   I see **an** apple.

2. Both are used with singular countable nouns only.

    a. I use one cup.   I use a cup.

    b. I use one orange.   I use an orange.

    c. I use sugar.   I use sugar.

3. Use "an" to verify whether to use "a" or "an" with a countable noun.

    a. an <u>umbrella</u>   b. ~~an~~ <u>unicorn</u>
        a e i o u   ~~a e i o u~~

4. "A" and "an" mean "one not special ~".

    a. I want an olive. (one not special olive)

    b. I want a black olive. (one not special black olive)

    c. I want a very green olive. (one not special very green olive)

                  a _____   an _____
                                                                       a e i o u

"A" AND "AN"

Let's play the "a" and "an" game!

Match "a" or "an" with the letters.

a _____

an _____
ah, eh, ih, oh, uh

I   see

__ A a	__ G g	__ M m	__ S s	__ Y y
__ B b	__ H h	__ N n	__ T t	__ Z z
__ C c	__ I i	__ O o	__ U u	
__ D d	__ J j	__ P p	__ V v	
__ E e	__ K k	__ Q q	__ W w	
__ F f	__ L l	__ R r	__ X x	

THE

"The" are very easy to comprehend and use.

1. "The" is used with singular and plural nouns.

>I see the trees.

>I see sugar.

2. Use "the" when a noun or nouns are special to you. If it is not special to you, omit it.

   I want the tree, not roses.

   I want the books, not a magazine.

3. "The" is used in "special" cases where the noun is either singular or plural.

   A. I want a pen.

   B. Here you are.

   A. I did not want a "red" pen. I wanted the "black ball point" pen.

   B. Next time, be specific and say that you want a "black ball point" pen.

"The" means "1, 2, 3, 4 ~ ∞ special ~".

   a. I want an olive. (one not special olive)
   b. I want the olives. (2, 3, 4 ~ ∞ special olives)
   c. I want my olive. (one very special olive)

Some equivalents of "the" are "my, your, our, his, her, its" and "their. They make the nouns more personal (special) to the speaker.

THE
WHICH DO YOU WANT?

I want **the** ___ not **the** _____. chair   stool

I want **the** ___ not **the** _____. red sock   blue sock

I want **the** ___ not **the** _____. fruits   potato

I want **the** ___ not **the** _____. crayon   books

I want **the** ___ not **the** _____. glasses   cups

PUT YOUR HANDS....

1. Put your hands above your head.

2. Put your hands next to you.

3. Put your hands in front of you.

4. Put your hands behind you.

5. Put your hands on your head.

6. Put your hands on your shoulders.

PUT YOUR HANDS....

7. Put your hands on your waist.

8. Put your hands on your lap.

9. Put your hands on your feet.

10. Put your hand in your hand.

11. Take your hand out.

12. Put your hand on your hand.

13. Put your hand under your hand.

THE DAYS OF THE WEEK

Yesterday
(Before)

Today
(This)

Tomorrow
(After)

Monday Tuesday Wednesday Thursday Friday Saturday Sunday

Today is Tuesday. Tomorrow is _____. (Wednesday)	⇩ Tuesday	⇨ Wednesday
Tomorrow is Wednesday. Yesterday was _____. (Monday)	⇦ Monday	⇨ Wednesday
Yesterday was Monday. Today is _____. (Tuesday)	⇦ Monday	⇩ Tuesday
What is the day after tomorrow? The day after tomorrow is _____.	⇨	⇨ ?day
What was the day before yesterday? The day before yesterday was _____.	⇦ ?day	⇦
What was the day before Monday? The day before Monday was _____. (Sunday)	⇦ Sunday	Monday
What is the day after Sunday? The day after Sunday is _____. (Monday)	Sunday	⇨ Monday

Monday ~ Sunday = a week

Monday ~ Friday = the weekday

Saturday ~ Sunday = the weekend

THE DAYS OF THE WEEK

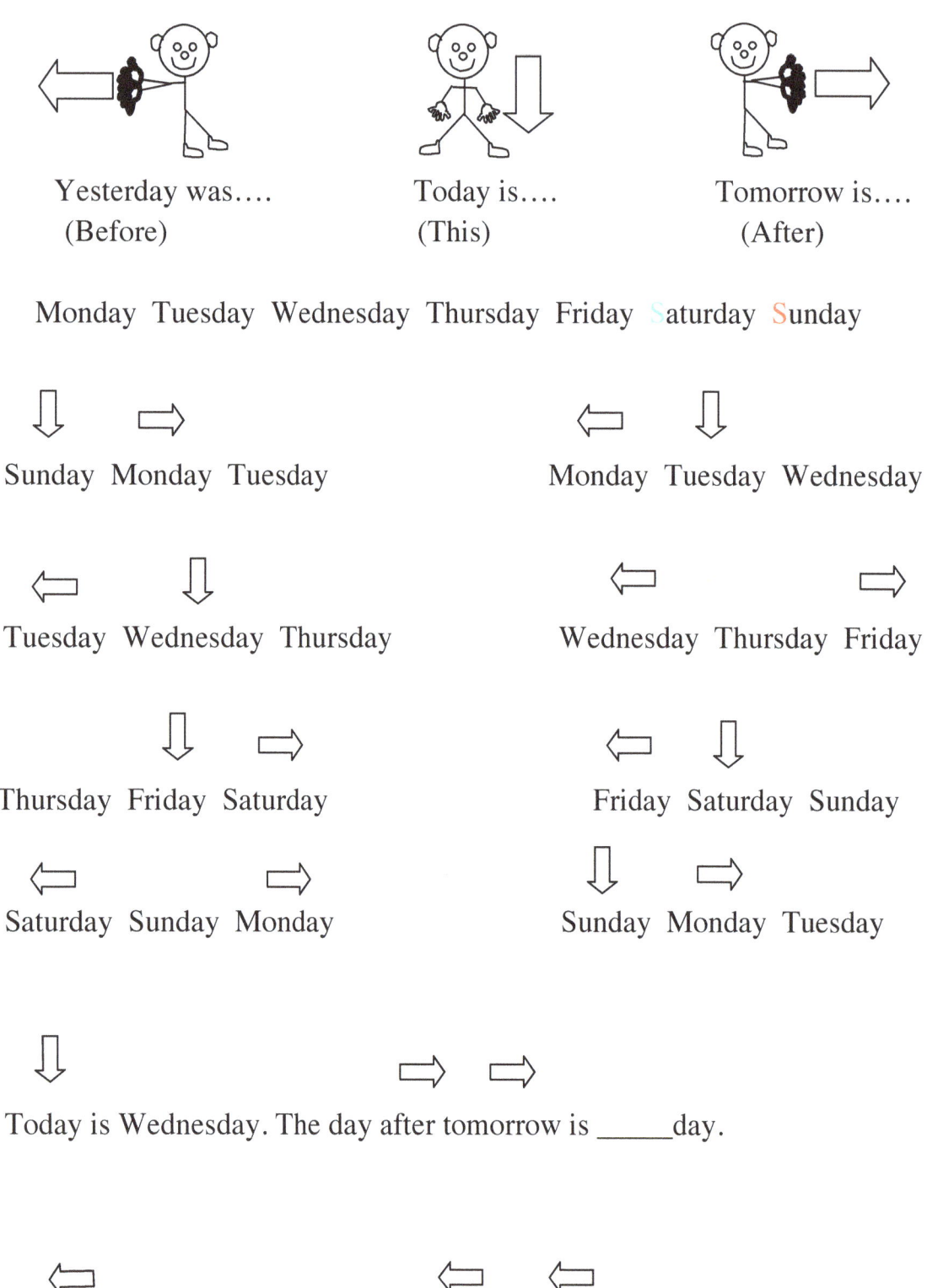

Today is Wednesday. The day after tomorrow is _____day.

Yesterday was Tuesday. The day before yesterday was _____day.

IN ORDER

1. Write from 1 to 10 in order.

2. Count from 1 to 10 in order.

3. Write the alphabet from A to Z in order.

4. Put the clock in order.

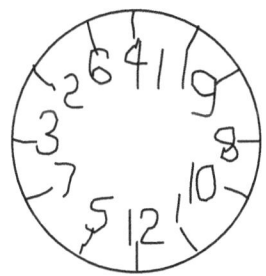 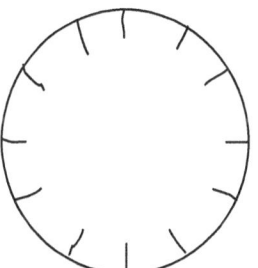

5. Put the face in order.

WHAT IS MISSING?
(PARTS)

1. A head is missing.

2. A 4 is missing.

3. The letter D is missing.

A, B, C,   , E, F, G....

4. A cup is missing.

5. A shoe is missing.

THE MONTHS OF THE YEAR

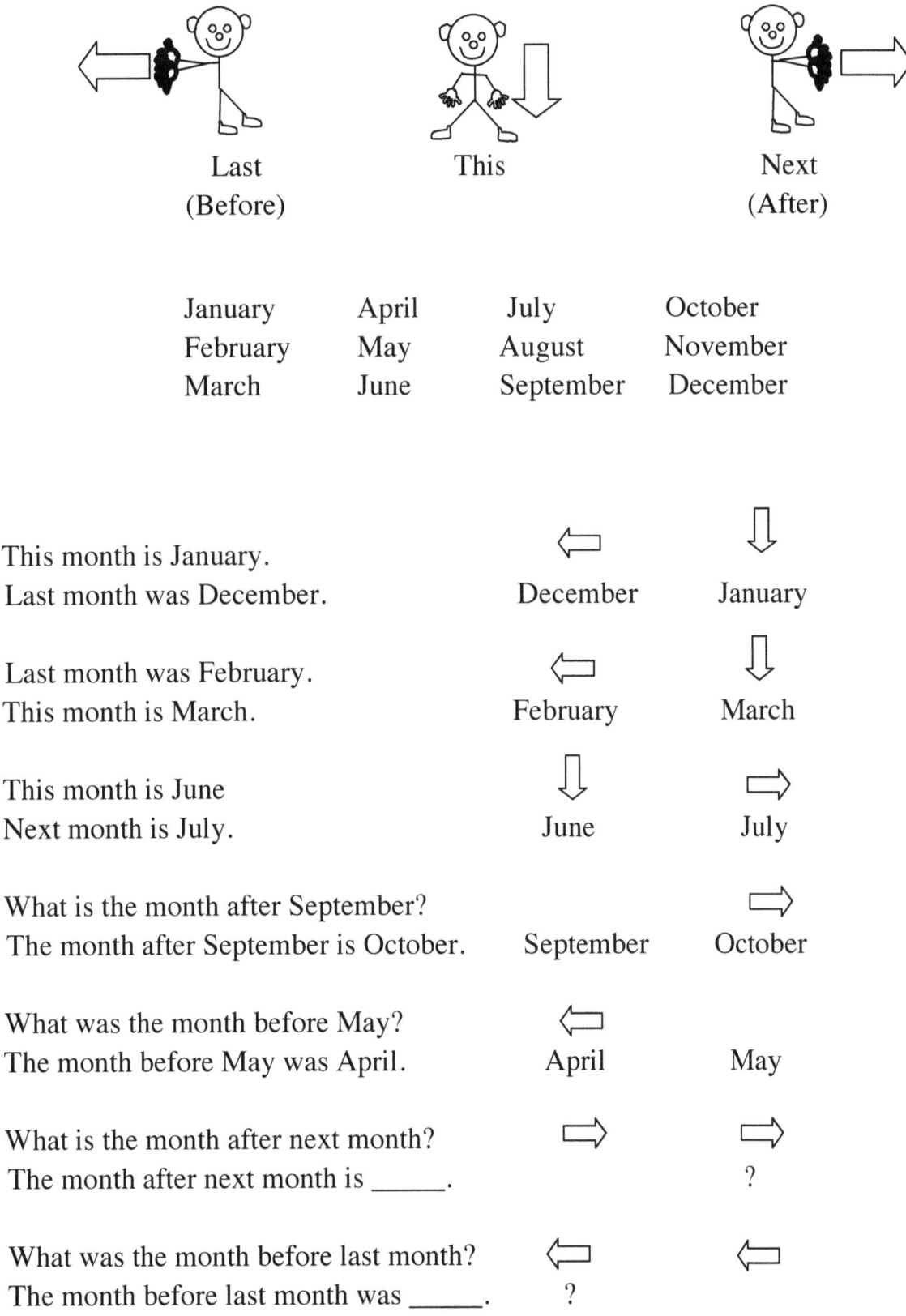

| Last | This | Next |
| (Before) | | (After) |

January   April   July   October
February May   August   November
March   June   September   December

This month is January.
Last month was December.

Last month was February.
This month is March.

This month is June
Next month is July.

What is the month after September?
The month after September is October.

What was the month before May?
The month before May was April.

What is the month after next month?
The month after next month is _____.

What was the month before last month?
The month before last month was _____.

There are 28 ~ 31 days in a month. There are 12 months in a year.

11

THE MONTHS OF THE YEAR

Last (Before) This Next (After)

January   April   July   October
February   May   August   November
March   June   September December

January February March   April May June

July August September   October November December

This month is November.   Next month is _____.

Last month was January.   Next month is _____.

This month is February.   The month before last month was _____.

This month is April.   The month after next month is _____

What is the month after May?   May   _____

What was the month before December?   _____ December

THE TRAVELS OF THE EARTH

As the earth, spins it rotates around the sun also.

1 spin = day

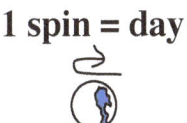

7 spins = 1 week

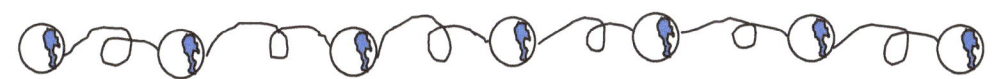

Monday   Tuesday   Wednesday   Thursday   Friday   Saturday   Sunday

28 ~ 31 spins = 1 month

JANUARY FEBRUARY MARCH APRIL MAY JUNE JULY
AUGUST SEPTEMBER OCTOBER NOVEMBER DECEMBER

1 rotation = 365.25 spins = 12 months = 1 year

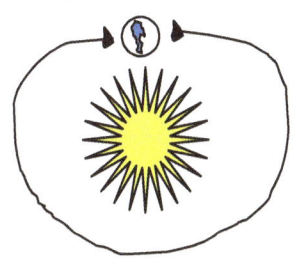

THE TRAVELS OF THE EARTH

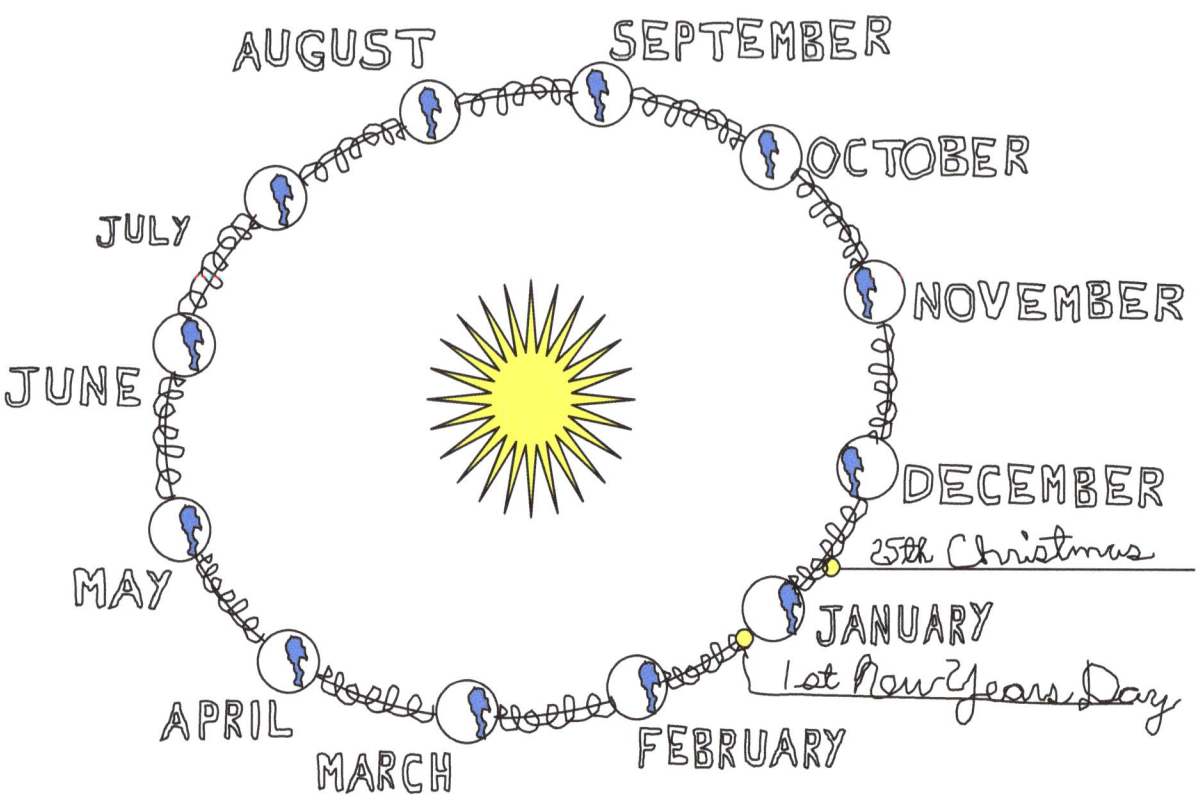

Today is Sunday.   The Earth spins 2 times. What day is it?   _____

Today is Monday. The Earth spins 1 time.   What day is it?   _____

Today is Friday.   The Earth spins 3 times. What day is it?   _____

Today is Thursday. If the Earth spins 2 times what day is it?   _____

Yesterday was Tuesday. How many times did the Earth spin? _____

How many spins is your age?   _____

How many rotations are you?   _____

When is your birthday?   _____

Write in your birthday on the map.

WHAT ARE YOU DOING?

1. I am putting my shoe on.

2. I am showering.

3. I am bathing.

4. I am singing.

5. I am crying.

WHAT ARE YOU DOING?

1. I am putting my shoe on.

   _____

2. I am showering.

   _____

3. I am bathing.

_____

4. I am singing.

   _____

5. I am crying.

   _____

WHAT DID YOU DO?

1. I rode my bike.

_____

2. I washed clothes.

_____

3. I sliced a banana.

_____

4. I tore the paper.

_____

5. I kicked the ball.

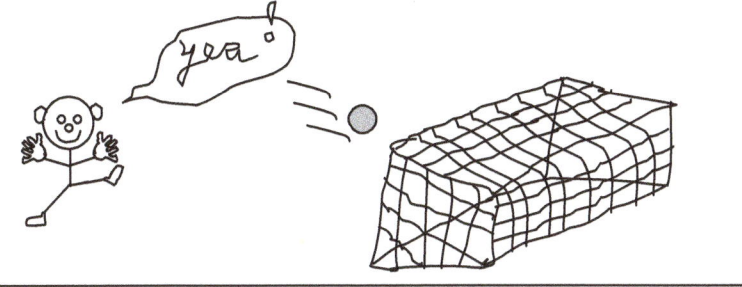

_____

WHAT DID YOU DO?

1. I rode my bike.

   _____

2. I washed clothes.

   _____

3. I sliced a banana.

   _____

4. I tore the paper.

   _____

5. I kicked the ball.

   _____

WHAT WILL YOU DO?

1. I will skate.

 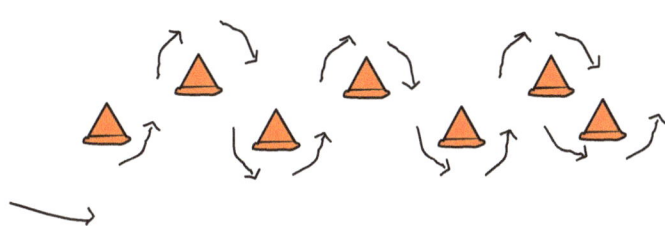

2. I will read.

3. I will talk.

 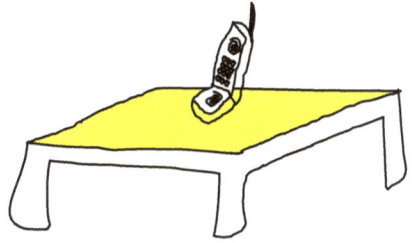

4. I will sleep.

 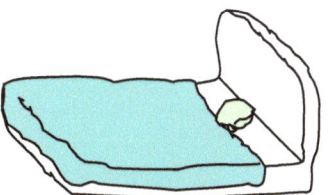

5. I will vacuum.

WHAT WILL YOU DO?

1. I will skate.

   _____

2. I will read.

   _____

3. I will talk.

   _____

4. I will sleep.

   _____

5. I will vacuum.

   _____

WHERE ARE YOU GOING?

1. I am going to the store.

   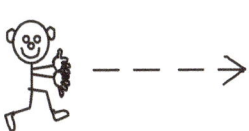 

2. I am going to school.

3. I am going home.

4. I am going to the bathroom.

     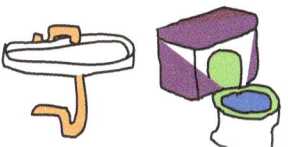

5. I am going to the kitchen.

    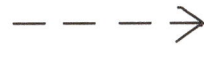 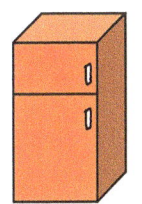 

6. I am going to my room.

WHERE ARE YOU GOING?

1. I am going to school.

2. I am going to the store.

3. I am going home.

4. I am going to the bathroom.

5. I am going to the kitchen.

6. I am going to my room.

WHERE DID YOU GO?

1. I went to the store.

2. I went to school.

3. I went home.

4. I went to the bathroom.

5. I went to the kitchen.

6. I went to my room.

23

WHERE DID YOU GO?

1. I went to the store.

2. I went to school.

3. I went home.

4. I went to the bathroom.

5. I went to the kitchen.

6. I went to my room.

WHERE WILL YOU GO?

1. I will go to the store.

2. I will go to school.

3. I will go home.

4. I will go to the bathroom.

5. I will go to the kitchen.

6. I will go to my room.

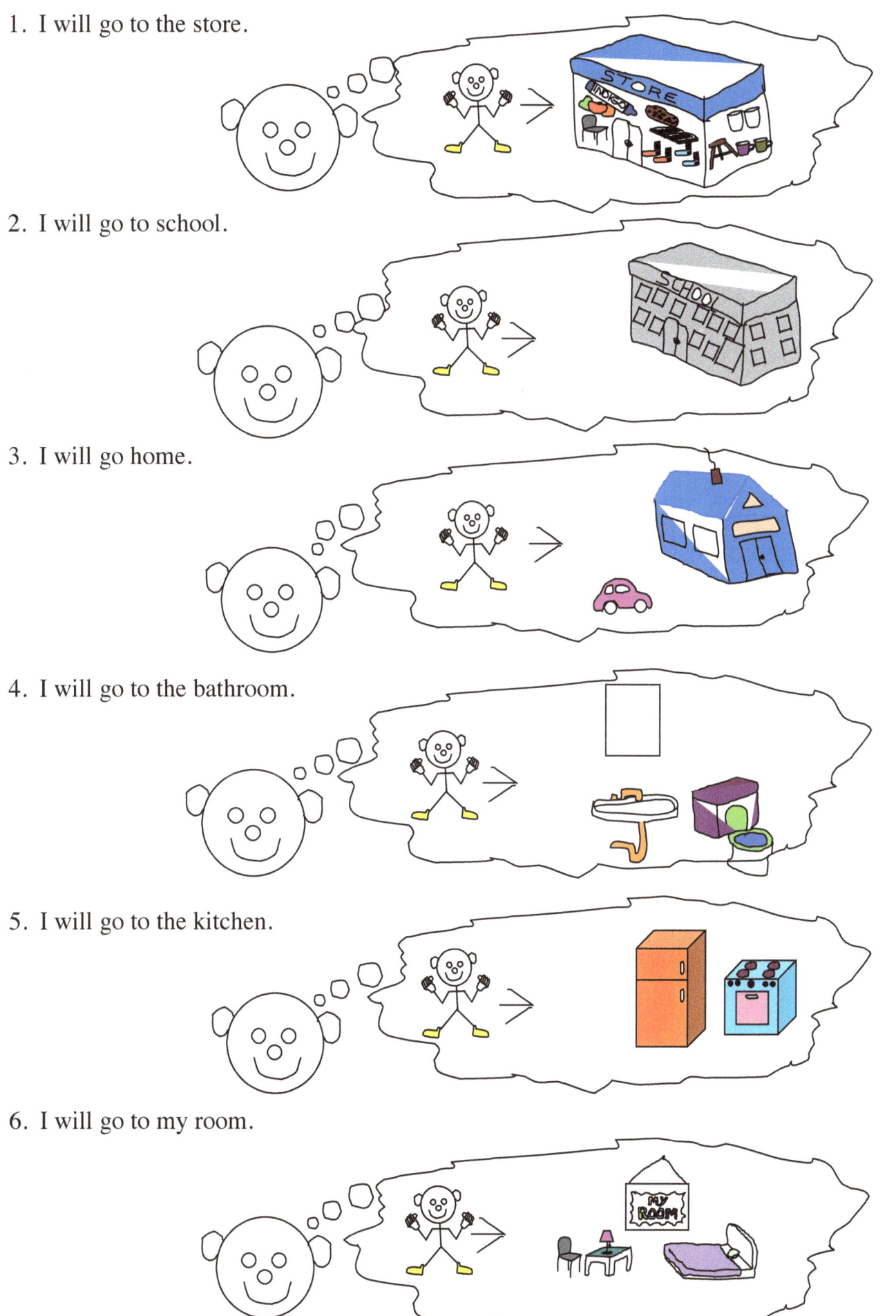

WHERE WILL YOU GO?

1. I will go to the store.

2. I will go to school.

3. I will go home.

4. I will go to the bathroom.

5. I will go to the kitchen.

6. I will go to my room.

HOW MANY SIDES?

1. How many sides does a triangle have?   A triangle has 3 sides.

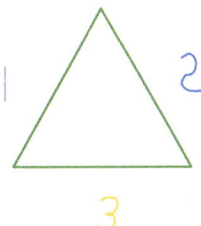

2. How many sides does a rectangle have? A rectangle has 4 sides.

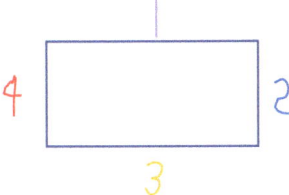

3. How many sides does a square have?   A square has 4 sides.

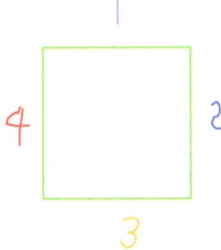

4. How many sides does a circle have?   A circle has no sides.

5. How many sides do you have?   I have many sides.

HOW MANY SIDES?

1. Draw your happy face.

2. Draw your sad face.

3. Draw your angry face.

4. Draw your sleepy face.

5. Draw your funny face.

WHERE ARE YOU?

1. I am in the bathroom.

2. I am outside.

3. I am in my room.

4. I am in the kitchen.

5. I am in the dining room.

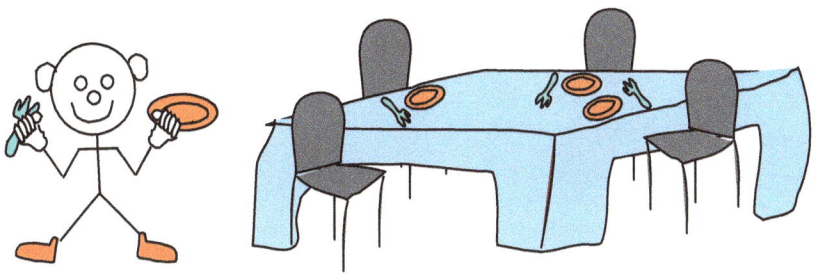

WHERE ARE YOU?

1. I am in the ___.

2. I am ___.

3. I am in my ___.

4. I am in the ___.

   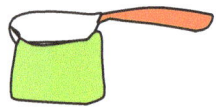

5. I am in the ___.

    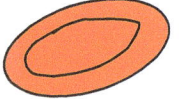

A. room

B. dining room

C. outside

D. bathroom

E. kitchen

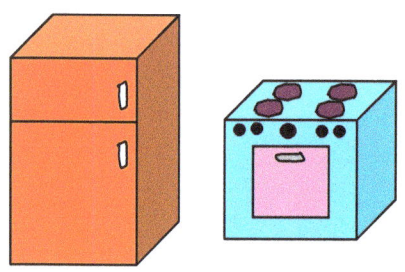

WHAT DO I NEED?

1. You need a ball.

2. You need a phone.

3. You need a pen.

4. You need a bed.

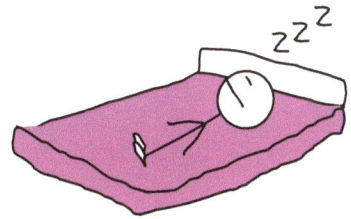

5. You need a chair.

WHAT DO I NEED?

1. You need a ball.

2. You need a phone.

3. You need a pen.

4. You need a bed.

5. You need a chair.

WHY ARE YOU ___?
BECAUSE, I AM ___.

1. CRYING?    SAD.

2. EATING?    HUNGRY.

3. DRINKING? 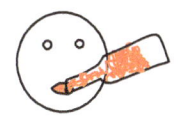   THRISTY.

4. IN BED? 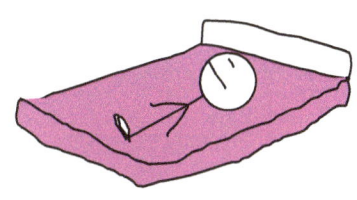   SLEEPING.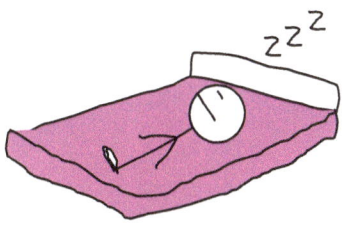

5. HAPPY?    EATING CAKE.

WHY ARE YOU ___?
BECAUSE, I AM ___.

1. CRYING?   SAD.

2. EATING?   HUNGRY.

3. DRINKING?   THIRSTY.

4. IN BED?   SLEEPING.

5. HAPPY?   EATING CAKE.

WHAT ARE YOU GOING TO DO?

1. I am going to play with my friends.

2. I am going to ride my bike.

3. I am going to fish in the lake.

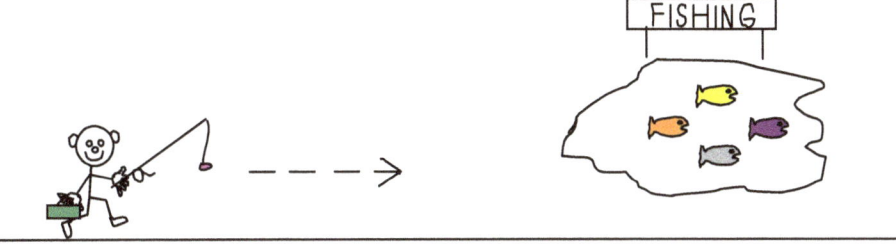

4. I am going to read books.

5. I am going to sit in the chair.

WHAT ARE YOU GOING TO DO?

1. I am going to play with my friends.

   _____

2. I am going to ride my bike.

   _____

3. I am going to fish in the lake.

   _____

4. I am going to read books.

   _____

5. I am going to sit in the chair.

   _____

WHAT WILL YOU GO DO?

1. I will go play with my friends.

2. I will go ride my bike.

3. I will go fish in the lake.

4. I will go read books.

5. I will go sit in the chair.

6. I will go eat fruits.

WHAT WILL YOU GO DO?

1. I will go play with my friends.

2. I will go ride my bike.

3. I will go fish in the lake.

4. I will go read books.

5. I will go sit in the chair.

6. I will go eat fruit.

WHAT DID YOU GO DO?

1. I went to play with my friends.

2. I went to ride my bike.

3. I went to fish in the lake.

4. I went to read books.

5. I went to sit in the chair.

6. I went to eat fruit.

WHAT DID YOU GO DO?

1. I went to play with my friends.

2. I went to ride my bike.

3. I went to fish in the lake.

4. I went to read books.

5. I went to sit in the chair.

6. I went to eat fruit.

WHAT DO YOU DO ON ____DAY?

1. I play tennis on Monday.

2. I play baseball on Tuesday.

3. I play volleyball on Wednesday.

4. I play with my friends on Thursday.

5. I ride my bike on Friday.

6. I wash clothes on Saturday.

7. I sleep on Sunday.

WHAT DO YOU DO ON ____DAY?

1. I play tennis on Monday.

2. I play baseball on Tuesday.

3. I play volleyball on Wednesday.

4. I play with my friends on Thursday.

5. I ride my bike on Friday.

6. I wash clothes on Saturday.

7. I sleep on Sunday.

WHERE IS THE _____ (AT)?
(SINGULAR PT. 1)

1. The pillow <u>is</u> <u>on</u> my bed.

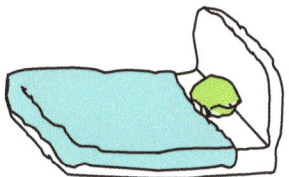

2. The phone <u>is</u> <u>under</u> the chair.

3. The picture <u>is</u> <u>in</u> my room.

4. The dog <u>is</u> <u>outside of</u> the house.

5. The key <u>is</u> <u>in front of</u> the lamp.

WHERE IS THE _____ (AT)?
(SINGULAR PT. 1)

1. The pillow is _____ my bed.

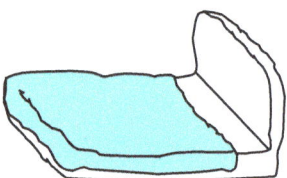

2. The phone is _____ the chair.

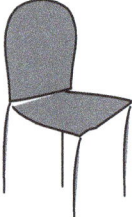

3. The picture is _____ my room.

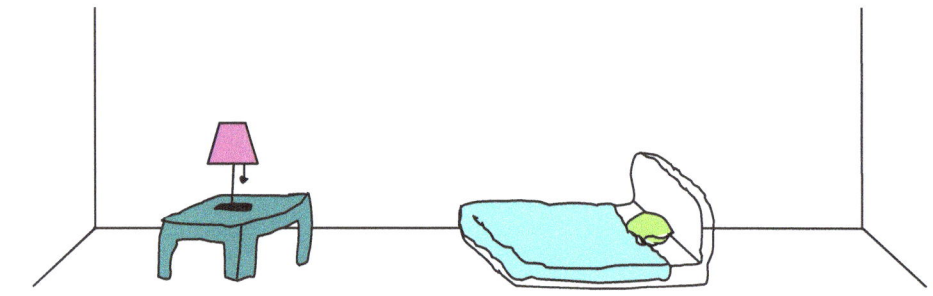

4. The dog is _____ the house.

5. The key is _____ the lamp.

WHERE ARE THE _____ (AT)?
(PLURAL PT. 1)

1. The cups are behind the fruit.

2. The skates are next to the boots.

3. The crayons are above the sink.

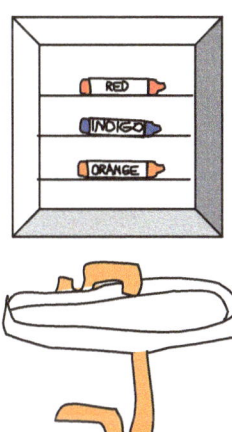

4. The keys are near the book

5. The dogs are far from the house

WHERE ARE THE _____ (AT)?
(PLURAL PT. 1)

1. The cups are behind the fruit.

2. The skates are next to the boots.

3. The crayons are above the sink.

4. The keys are near the book.

5. The dogs are far from the house.

WHERE IS THE _____ (AT)?
(SINGULAR PT. 2)

1. The red crayon <u>is</u> <u>inside</u> the cabinet.

2. The apple <u>is</u> <u>between</u> the pear and the orange

3. The phone <u>is</u> <u>underneath</u> the chair.

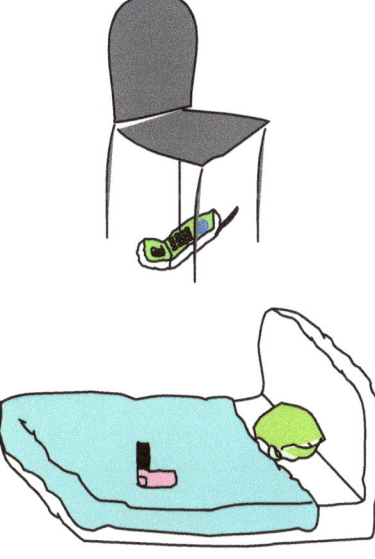

4. The sock <u>is</u> <u>on top of</u> the blanket.

5. The car <u>is</u> <u>around</u> the corner.

47

WHERE IS THE _____ (AT)?
(SINGULAR   PT. 2)

1. The red crayon <u>is</u> <u>inside of</u> the cabinet.

2. The apple <u>is</u> <u>between</u> the pear and the orange

3. The phone <u>is</u> <u>underneath</u> the chair.

4. The sock <u>is</u> <u>on top of</u> the blanket.

5. The car <u>is</u> <u>around</u> the corner.

WHERE ARE THE _____ (AT)?
(PLURAL PT. 2)

1. The socks <u>are</u> <u>on top of</u> the blanket.

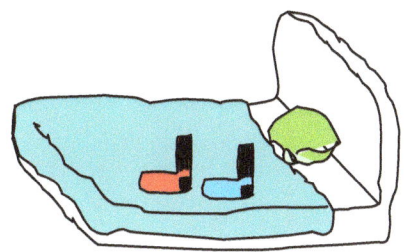

2. The crayons <u>are</u> <u>inside of</u> the book.

3. The keys <u>are</u> <u>beneath</u> the chair.

4. The glasses <u>are</u> <u>beside</u> the remote control.

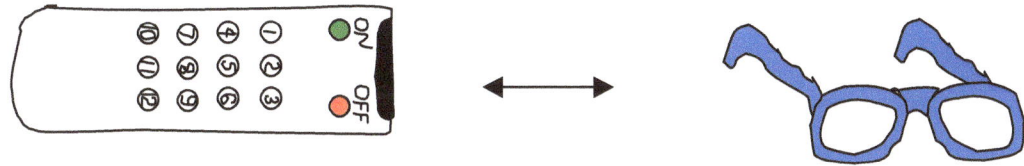

5. The forks <u>are</u> <u>above</u> the cups.

WHERE ARE THE _____ (AT)?
(PLURAL PT. 2)

1. The socks <u>are</u> <u>on top of</u> the blanket.

2. The crayons <u>are</u> <u>inside</u> of the book.

3. The keys <u>are</u> <u>beneath</u> the chair.

4. The glasses <u>are</u> <u>beside</u> the remote control.

5. The forks <u>are</u> <u>above</u> the cups.

WHAT IS MISSING?
(LETTERS)

a p ___ l e

h o u ___ e

c a ___

___ o r k

c ___ p

b e ___

s h o w ___ r

s i ___ g

t r ___ a ___ g ___ e

___ a p p y

DO YOU LIKE _____?

1. Do you like dogs?   Yes, I like dogs.

2. Do you like sharks?   No, I don't like sharks.

3. Do you like boats?

 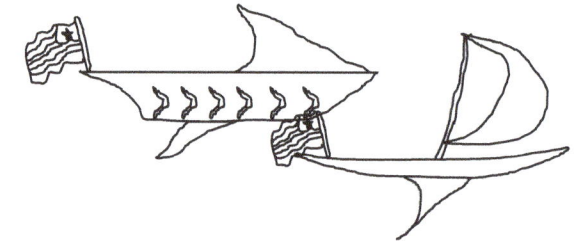

4. Do you like chili peppers?   No, I don't like chili peppers.

5. Do you like fruit?   Yes, I like fruit.

 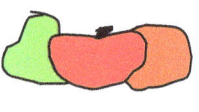

6. Do you like math?   Yes, I love math.

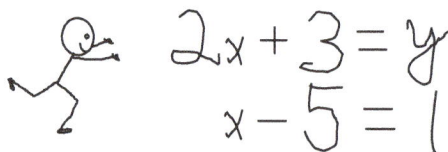

DO YOU LIKE _____?

1. Do you like dogs?   Yes, I like dogs.

2. Do you like sharks?   No, I don't like sharks.

3. Do you like boats?   Yes, I like boats.

4. Do you like chili peppers?   No, I don't like chili peppers.

5. Do you like fruit?   Yes, I like fruit.

6. Do you like math?   Yes, I like math.

BASIC QUESTIONS

1. What is your name?

2. How are you?

3. How old are you?

4. Where do you live?

5. How many brothers and sisters do you have?

6. What school do you go to?

7. What grade are you in?

8. Do you like your teacher?

9. How many friends do you have?

10. How is the weather?

BASIC QUESTIONS

1.

2.

3.

4.

5.

6.

7.

8.

9.

10.

"WHAT" AND "WHO"

1. Who am I? You are a n__rse.

2. Who are you? I am _____.

3. Who are they? They are pe __ ple.

4. What is this? This is a c__ __ __.

5. What are these? These are ca__d__es.

6. What is it? It is a __efri__erato__.

7. What are they? They are f__r__iture.

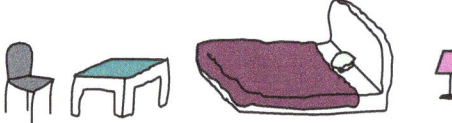

www.ingramcontent.com/pod-product-compliance
Lightning Source LLC
Chambersburg PA
CBHW042302010526
44113CB00047B/2769